Rebekah
THE MOTHER OF TWINS

The Story of Rebekah
accurately retold from the Bible
by
CARINE MACKENZIE

Design and Illustrations
Duncan McLaren

Published in Great Britain by
CHRISTIAN FOCUS PUBLICATIONS LTD
Geanies House, Fearn, Tain, Ross-shire IV20 1TW, Scotland

© 1985 Christian Focus Publications Ltd ISBN 0 906731 45 3

Published in Australia and New Zealand by
DAYSTAR and distributed by W. A. BUCHANAN & CO
20 Morrisby Street, Geebung, Brisbane, Q., 4034, Australia

© 1985 DAYSTAR ISBN 0 949925 14 4

New edition 1989

Rebekah was a beautiful girl who grew up with her brother Laban in the land of Padanaram, which we now call Syria. She was a good and dutiful daughter and helped her father Bethuel and her mother with the household tasks.

One of her daily duties was to fetch water for the house from the well. Each evening she would go to the well with a pitcher or big jug on her shoulder.

One evening Rebekah went to the well as usual. Just as she finished filling her jug, a man came near. 'Please let me drink a little water from your jug,' he said.

'Drink, my Lord,' Rebekah replied politely and quickly gave him some water. When the man had drunk enough to satisfy his thirst, Rebekah said to him, 'I will draw water for your camels too.' Rebekah worked hard, drawing from the well as much water as the thirsty camels could drink.

When the camels had finished drinking, the man gave Rebekah a valuable gift — a gold earring and two gold bracelets. 'Please tell me whose daughter you are,' he said. 'Would there be room in your father's house for me and my men to stay for the night?' Rebekah replied, 'I am Bethuel's daughter. Of course, we have enough straw for your camels, plenty of food for you and your men and enough room for you to stay.'

The man bowed his head and prayed to God. He believed and was thankful that God was guiding him in his journey and helping him to do his job.

You too can ask God to help you
with your work. Remember to
thank him when he does help you.

Rebekah ran home ahead of the man to tell her family to prepare for some guests.

When brother Laban saw Rebekah's beautiful gifts he knew that the visitor was someone special. He rushed out to welcome him. 'Come in,' he said, 'everything is ready for you.'

The visitor washed his feet which would be dusty after travelling. Then a meal was set down before him. But he said, 'I will not eat anything until I have told you why I am here.'

'My master Abraham has sent me from the land of Canaan back to his native land to find a suitable wife for his son Isaac. He assured me that the Lord God would guide me all the way. So I asked the Lord for a sign.

If a girl came, who would give me water and also offer to give water to my camels, I would know that she was the right girl for Isaac.

'No sooner had I said this,' the man continued, 'when Rebekah came down to the well and gave me and the camels all the water we needed. When I asked about her family I was so thankful to learn that the Lord had guided me to the family of my master's brother. Will you agree to Rebekah becoming Isaac's wife?'

Laban and Bethuel both agreed
that God had arranged everything.
They could not find any fault. 'We
will allow Rebekah to become your
master's son's wife,' they said.

The man bowed down and
worshipped God. He then brought
out gold and silver jewels and
lovely clothes for Rebekah and her
family. Only when his work was
done, did he sit down and enjoy
his evening meal.

The visitor stayed with Bethuel overnight and in the morning he was anxious to start the return trip to Canaan. Laban and his mother were sad to see Rebekah leaving them so soon. 'Let her stay for a few days yet, at least ten,' they said. But the servant was keen to get back to his master with the good news. 'Let's ask Rebekah herself,' they said. 'Will you go with this man?' they asked. 'I will go,' she replied firmly.

God is also asking you a question. Will you follow the Lord Jesus and love him? What is your answer?

Rebekah started out on her new life that very day. Her only companion was her nurse Deborah. She left her family and her home and made the journey to a strange land to marry a man she had never seen. This was God's plan and purpose for her life.

Your life is in God's hand. He has a plan for you too.

One evening Isaac was out in the peace and quiet of the field thinking and praying to God. When he looked up he saw a train of camels coming near. When Rebekah noticed this young man she asked the servant who he was. 'That is my master Isaac,' she was told. She jumped down from the camel and after covering her face with a veil, as was the custom, she walked to meet Isaac. The servant informed Isaac about all that had happened. Isaac loved Rebekah very much and they were married right away. Rebekah was a great comfort to Isaac whose mother Sarah had recently died.

Isaac and Rebekah were married for nearly twenty years but they still had no baby boy or girl. Isaac prayed to God and asked him to give them a child. God heard his prayer and Rebekah was soon expecting — not one baby but twins. Before they were born, Rebekah asked God about her expected children. God told her that her sons would be two different nations and that the younger one would be more important than the elder one.

Rebekah's twin sons were very different in appearance. Esau was born first. He was red and quite hairy. His brother Jacob was smooth-skinned.

As Esau was older he would have
certain privileges known as his
birthright including a special
blessing from his father.

As the boys grew up they were still very different in their appearance and their interests. Esau loved being out in the country, hunting wild animals and bringing home venison for his father to eat. But Jacob had a quieter nature and preferred to stay closer to home. He was his mother's favourite.

One day Esau came home from hunting absolutely starving. Jacob had been cooking and Esau could smell the lovely aroma of hot lentil soup. 'Give me some of your soup, please, I am nearly fainting,' said Esau. 'I shall give you food, if you will agree to give me your birthright,' replied Jacob.

'I am dying of hunger,' gasped Esau. 'Of what use is my birthright to me?' So the agreement was made. Esau got some bread and lentil soup: and Jacob received the birthright.

One day Rebekah overheard a conversation between Esau and his father Isaac who was now growing blind. 'I am getting old,' Isaac said, 'and I do not know when I may die. Take your bow and arrow, Esau, and go out and hunt. Bring back some venison to make my favourite meal. After I eat it, I will bless you before I die.'

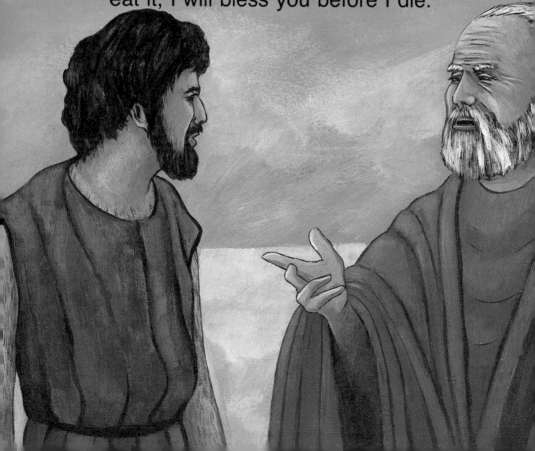

As soon as Esau had departed on his hunting trip, Rebekah hurried to find Jacob. 'Now do what I tell you, Jacob,' she said. 'Go to the flock and bring me two good young goat kids: I will make a tasty dish, just the way your father likes it. After he has eaten he will bless you instead of Esau.' Was she remembering what God had told her years before about the younger son being more important than the older?

'But Esau has a hairy skin and I am smooth,' objected Jacob. 'If father finds out that I am deciving him, he will probably curse me, and not bless me.' But Rebekah urged Jacob. 'Just do as I say. If there is any curse, it will be on me.'

So Jacob did as Rebekah wanted. Soon the lovely savoury meat was ready. Rebekah took some of Esau's best clothes and helped Jacob dress in them. Then she took the skins of the kids which had been used to make the stew and covered Jacob's hands and neck. They did not feel so smooth now. They felt rough and hairy — more like Esau's.

Jacob went to Isaac's tent with the meat and some bread. 'My father,' he said. 'Who is that,' replied the blind Isaac. 'I am Esau your first born son,' lied Jacob. 'I have done as you asked. Come and eat this venison, and bless me.'

'How did you manage to find it so quickly, my son?' asked Isaac.

'The Lord God brought it to me,' continued Jacob. Jacob sinned when he told lies. If you tell a lie that is also a sin. Often one lie leads to another.

Isaac was not sure, so he said,
'Come a little nearer to me so that
I can feel if it really is Esau.' Jacob
must have been scared. Rebekah
must have been anxious too,
wondering what was happening.
Isaac was puzzled. 'The voice
sounds like Jacob but the hands
feel like Esau,' he said.

So Jacob and Rebekah's trick was not found out. After Isaac had eaten the meal Jacob came and kissed his father, and Isaac blessed Jacob, asking God to provide for and make him prosper.

Almost as soon as Jacob had left his father, brother Esau came back from his hunting trip. He prepared the venison stew and brought it to his father. 'Who are you?' exclaimed Isaac. 'I am Esau, of course,' he replied. Isaac was quite taken aback. 'Then who has just been here and given me venison stew and received my blessing — and indeed will be blessed?' Esau was heart broken when he heard this. 'Can you not bless me too, father?' he begged. 'My brother has taken away my birthright and now my blessing too.'

Isaac answered, 'I have said that he will be lord over his brother and that will come to pass.' Esau hated his brother for this and vowed to kill him.

When Rebekah heard this she called for Jacob and said, 'Esau is planning to kill you. You had better escape to Haran. My brother Laban will give you a place to live. Once Esau's anger has cooled down, I will send for you.'

Isaac agreed with Rebekah and urged Jacob to go to his mother's old home.

Jacob had many adventures in the years that followed. Many years later he met with Esau again and made peace. When Jacob returned with his large family, Isaac was still living. Rebekah never saw her favourite son Jacob again. She died and was buried in a cave in a field called Machpelah.

Rebekah and Jacob were very close but even the closest human friends must part one day. If you have the Lord Jesus Christ as your friend, he will never leave you nor forsake you. He is the best friend you could ever have.